The Poetry of Emotion

An Insane Roots Series

Tiffany Rochelle

Contents

Dedication

I would like to dedicate this book to anyone suffering.
Please know you are not alone.
And try to remember, there is great wisdom born from being broken.

Special Thanks

A special thank you to Kerry Fina, who first suggested I put together such a book many years ago. I have finally found the courage to take your advice.

To my childhood friend and spiritual teacher, Brittany Forrester, thank you for helping me find the spirit I needed to share my depth with the world.

To everyone who has supported me and shared in my journey, I appreciate you more than you will ever know. You keep me going, give me purpose and have helped me find fulfillment in so many ways.

Opening Thoughts

Much like everything I write, the pieces within this book are pieces of me, drawn from moments in my life when I knew no other way to process my emotions, but to pour them on the page.
And so, although at times you may feel as though you are traveling through the very darkest tunnels of my mind (and you are), I urge you to remember these as passing moments. More importantly, a necessary darkness that brought me to the clarity I feel today.

My inspiration for this series grew from a seed planted by step father, Kerry, many years ago. I always wanted to do it, but in all honesty, I lacked the courage. Until now! Poetry is such a sensitive form of expression for me and as you can imagine, I have suffered a wide variety of difficulties in my life (as have most of us) and over the years, I have found it necessary to sometimes surrender to the spiral of darkness in order to fully work through whatever it was and move forward.

Written loosely in the stages of grief, each piece shares a glimpse at the inner struggles of a child left behind, still searching after all these years for the desperately needed reassurance and security that had been taken away so long ago. It will take a deep look at the emotional roller coaster of depression and the strength it takes to overcome it. My hope is that this will help bring those struggling with similar toxic family dynamics and depression/anxiety together and more importantly to raise awareness of just how many people suffer from mental health issues, but are afraid to divulge them out of shame and humility.

It took me a long time to become brave enough to speak up for myself and I know I am not alone. The time has come to shed the shame surrounding anxiety & depression and find pride in having survived it. Even if you still suffer from it, every step you take forward, is momentum to be proud of. You are not weak, you are strong! Perhaps stronger than most because the baseline for each day is lower than that of others. Try to remember that the next time you are struggling to move forward. There is no real cure for depression, but every day you push through it, is a day you survived it and I have found, that in itself to be fuel for each day to come!

There is great beauty in being broken. The darkness we overcome is like the shedding of a chrysalis. What remains is an empty shell of emotions, feelings we sometimes use as protection when we are spiraling out in a cycle of depression or anxiety, but once we work through this, we come out the other side anew; an even more beautiful you!

It's not all poetry though. Another one of my passions is photography and it too was an outlet for me in the past. And so, I have decided to implement some of my favorite shots throughout the book as well. So if you have ever wondered what really goes through this crazy noggin of mine, you are about to find out!

Hang on tight folks, you are about to take one mad ride!

Photo courtesy of Krista Boettcher

Love

Before I was blessed with my current partner, my relationship with love over the last ten years was one of mostly anguish and despair. For a very long time, I had a lot of trust issues, which grew stronger with every betrayal and failed attempt at love. I came to a point just before meeting my boyfriend where I honestly felt I was done with the prospect of ever finding someone. I resigned myself to the fact that maybe it just wasn't in the cards for me. And wouldn't you know, just when I had given up, out of nowhere, there he was!

All in and all I've ever wanted. My love, this poem is for you.

> **What Would It Feel Like to Have All You've Ever Wanted?**
> I stood there starring through the glass as I felt his arms wrap slowly around my waist
> Gazing out upon the life we built together
> It was the moment I had waited for all my life
> It was when I knew
> I truly had all I'd ever wanted

It was a long journey to here and as with many adventures, I came out the other side wiser for having experienced them. Wisdom I would like to share with you now. My hope being it may save someone else from making the same mistakes or less of them at least. After all, some mistakes are worth making. How else do we learn?

Let me start by asking, how many of you have been in love? I mean truly/unconditionally in love with another person? And if you don't know, than the answer is most likely NO. Because, let me tell you, you'd know.
Now, I've had it twisted myself at times, but once you feel it, I mean really feel it, nothing else compares. And that is not to say that every relationship I have been in has been with someone I was truly in love with either. In reviewing my many failed attempts at relationships, one thing became very clear: Either you feel it or you don't, it's that simple. All this BS about timing or not being ready is just that, BS.
When I think about my one great love in past, the timing was all wrong and neither of us were ready, but we didn't care. All that mattered to us was being together. Sure we had our share of disagreements, but at the end of the day, we never loved one another any less. Even to this day, there is never a question in my mind as to the in-penetrable bond between us. Sure the dynamic of our relationship/friendship has changed over the years, but that is a story for another day, let's just say we now share a common interest…men!

Anyway…I guess my point is that we all seem to make the search for love so much more difficult than it needs to be. We seem to find ourselves staying in relationships out of comfort, chasing all the wrong people or hanging on to a hope that someday it will all work out. And for what? Why?

The cold hard truth is that all the signs are usually right in front of us that it is not meant to be, but out of some need to be loved we keep chasing, we refuse to see them. Let's be honest, telling someone you are 'just not that into them' is a bit of an awkward conversation to have. We think we are doing right by saying something like, "it's not you, it's me" or "I am just not looking for anything serious right now". It is a way of letting them down easy without completely breaking their heart. Seems logical right? In my opinion…it's crap. Not all cases of 'course, there are some exceptions to the rule, but for the rest of us…is that really what we mean or is it just a way for us not to feel bad about telling someone we don't feel the same and we never will? I have been on both sides of this and neither are pleasant. Obviously, the side of rejection being the worst.

What I am about to say may come across as a bit harsh, but life lessons usually are. Love is blind and the need for it crippling. Which is why it is so important to learn to love yourself above all else.

You may be thinking that is easy for me to say, but remember, looks can be deceiving. I, too, harbor my own special set of demons. The path in conquering them has led me here, hopefully to impart some of the wisdom gained by my experiences to save someone else from some of the same struggles.

Okay, so like I said above…Rule #1 and the most important of them all! -Learn how to love yourself.

And I don't mean every second of every day, but you need to get to a point where your happiness does not depend on someone else. I think this is the biggest issue in relationships. There is this idea perpetuated in society that we need to find someone to complete us, or more insultingly save us. As a result we begin searching for this other half before we have even begun to understand who we are or what true love really is.

That is an awful lot of pressure to put on someone; your happiness. Not to mention it is an impossible task for anyone but yourself, so we are setting them up to disappoint us from the very beginning. Which they do, because they can't help not to and this continues to happen over and over again until the entire relationship unravels. Ask me how I know…

My New Year's resolution in 2015 was not only to learn to love myself, but to find myself. After all, it is hard to love someone you don't really know! And so the journey began. I started a new blog, moved to a new city and set the course for massive change.

It took almost two years, but by the start of 2017, I could confidently say I knew who I was, what I wanted, and most importantly, what I was worth! And for anyone who battles with depression, you know just how big of an accomplishment that was. I finally felt ready to give dating another try. It didn't pan out until just recently, but I learned two more very important lessons in the process.

1. No matter how much you grow as a person or how much you love yourself, being vulnerable with someone will always hold the potential of pain, but it also holds the possibility of finding what is truly meant to be. Tomorrow is not promised and if we never try, we will never know.

2. True love knows nothing of time. It will not wait for you to be ready or the timing to be right. Genuine, unconditional love between two destined souls has one goal and one goal alone…unity. You will not have to search for it, you will not have to chase it and you will not have to question it. If you are doing any of those three things, it is not meant to be.

And on that note, I will leave you with these parting words of wisdom on the subject of love. I hope they give you the courage to continue fighting and save you a bit of heartbreak along the way.

Please do yourself a favor, don't wait. Don't be afraid to try your hand at love. You may lose it all in the end, but then again it may be the best decision you ever made. Wouldn't it be better to know? And the next time you fall for someone and they tell you they are not looking for anything serious, remind yourself of what I have said.

And please know that what they most likely mean is… they are not looking for anything serious… with you. In all frankness, if they were to meet the right person tomorrow, do you really think there would be anything stopping them? Would there be anything stopping you? Exactly. Remember that.

Don't hang on to the possibility that one day they will change their mind and if you just hold on long enough, you will be the one they choose. Go live your life, they are. As much as it hurts, not everyone you love is going to love you back in the same way. It's not their fault and it's nothing you can change.

It either is or it isn't…that is all there is to it. Don't waste your time chasing something or someone that is almost what you want, you might end up overlooking the right one and wouldn't that be a shame.

Almost

I loved you. When it felt like I could never feel anything again, I felt you. And it almost saved me.

A Memory of Love

I awoke today to thoughts of you
Gentle and kind
Warming my heart
Just before sunrise

Despite the distance
It's as though you're right beside me

Keeping my eyes closed just a bit longer
Holding on tightly
To the memory of you

Extraordinarily Unusual

There is something about this thunder that seems to rattle my bones
Perhaps it is that I have always fantasized about kissing in the rain
Under the stars
Amidst the moonlight

Goosebumps begin to dance on my skin from the chill in the air
Or maybe it is the way he grazes my cheek in warming embrace

For a moment I am helpless, hopelessly falling...

His kiss is electric, pure lightning to my core and then I hear the rumble...
The thunder rising within us like an unstoppable flame

Never to be extinguished, no matter how we fight.

There is power in the clouds above,
Where the darkness unites our souls.

It is a place only the strange can see.

An extraordinarily unusual rift in time,
When we are fully exposed and perfectly understood.
A rarity for the peculiar, this, not having to pretend...to feel.

Love Tumble

Heartbeat, heartbeat break my fall

As I tumble into ecstasy

Below this sky

Above this earth

Rooted into being

As I never thought could be

A touch as if I've never felt before

A love, thought impossible

If Morning Never Comes...

An evening date with you my love shall take me to the heavens.
Within your arms, my crib, I lay.
My lullaby; your breathing.
The gentle beat of your sweet heart; the hope you'll always love me.
So whisper sweet and say goodnight, I'll see you in the morning.
Should daylight come and I not stir,
Please know sweet boy I love you.
With all my heart, with all my soul,
For all my life, I love you.

Imperfectly Perfect

I trace the lines of your face, struggling not to lose myself in your eyes.
But I do.
Every time.
There is no love for me there,
But it makes no difference to my heart.
You are not like the others.
And neither am I.
Perhaps that is why, I feel so safe with you.
And so empty when you are away.
If there was only a way to end this devotion.
A flaw,
I simply cannot overlook.
And so I search.
Reviewing our time together,
Looking for a reason,
To let it all go.

Appreciation

Life is about experience. All the little moments that make up our days are special in their own way and it is important that we find a way to value them.

In today's society everyone seems to be rushing to get to the finish line. Once they do is it really worth it if they missed the lessons along the way? After all, what is an accomplishment without the hard work that went in to achieving it? I guess what I am saying is enjoy the journey. Be eager, but not so much that you miss the collective moments along the path that took you there.

Allow yourself the time to appreciate what you have before reaching for what you don't. It is in this state of appreciation that you will find peace. A peace that will hold you together during times of hurt and disappointment and help you grow in moments of reflection.

And it is when you are at peace with where you are in any given moment that you will learn to allow yourself to feel, but then to let it go.

It is in this peaceful state of gratitude that I have found a love for myself that is nurturing and safe. Alleviating the need to constantly search for it in something or someone else. In times of sorrow, I spiral. In times of anger, I reflect.

And in times of joy and peace, I savor.

Morning Poetry

In the early hours of morning
When the dew dangles on the grass
And nature just begins to wake
I am at peace

The air is thickened with quiet
And my brain has barely stirred
Thrills of unknown excitement lay before me
As I open myself up to the day
No expectation
Only the full embrace of its conception

There is great power here

The power of now
The ability to appreciate
Not just the day
But each and every moment
For you never know
Which of those moments may change your life

Raw

Oh how sweet the wisdom in your eyes
Dripping the tears of the lonely
How beautiful you are when you cry
Raw
Real
And
True

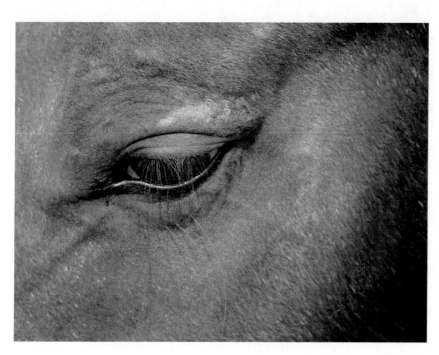

We Are One

There is such beauty in this moment
The hustle and bustle of people going by
A million thoughts running through their minds
Each motion individual
Yet intricately woven
Within this time and space
Strangers to one another in the physical
Though unknowingly connected
Within the unconsciousness of existence
Oh how beautiful
This power of now

What Joy

What joy
To lose yourself in a moment
To be fully present and aware
How peaceful
To experience all sensation around you
In this flutter of life
Freedom from expectation and circumstance
Content
If only for a moment

Anxiety

For me, anxiety and depression are like evil villains lurking in the shadows, ready to pounce on my good mood at any given moment. I never know when it will hit me or what the trigger will be. The only thing I do know for sure is that its visit is inevitable.

Every day before I open my eyes, I take the first thought that comes to mind and should it be a negative one, I take a deep breath and say to myself, "Not today" and then I reach for the closest positive thought I can find. And I continue to do that until I have moved my train of thought over to something or someone that makes me smile. If that doesn't work (and sometimes it doesn't), I may surrender to the moment, but as soon as I have a chance to release those emotions, I take it.

Whether that be writing, painting or simply taking some time to blubber about it, we all need an outlet. I have a friend who whenever they get upset, they go running and I have another friend who whenever they get upset, they go for a drive.

The point is, we are all human and part of being human means that we are emotional beings. There is nothing we can do to change that. And emotions are meant to be expressed. It is when they are not that we find ourselves spinning out of control.

Which is why having a support system or at least one person who knows you as well as (if not more than) you know yourself, is detrimental in winning the fight. We all need that one person who is understanding and supportive, but also not afraid to call us out when the need arises! Something I think we all need every once in a while.

The minute you turn from the ones who care for you, you surrender completely to whatever it is that is causing you to feel that way. Whether it is a person, a problem or an illness, when you turn away from the world and crawl inside yourself, you are giving up your power to change your circumstance. Maybe this will only last a few months, but there is always a chance of permanence. Darkness in a world full of color. The longer you spend in the dark, the harder it becomes to find the light. Why?

Because every thought you think, results in an emotion and every emotion another thought that leads to another emotion...you get the point. So when we wallow and believe me, I can be the queen of wallowing sometimes, we begin to validate the negativity we are experiencing.

The story we tell ourselves is incredibly important. It forms the way we see the world and ourselves. As well as determines what we attract into our current reality. This was a huge revelation I had back in 2016 and it has been my savior over the past few years when it comes to pulling myself back from the downward spiral of emotions that can pull me away from my path.

I have not yet mastered the art and perhaps I never will, but at least I'm trying. And some part of it must be working, because I am seeing evidence of it more and more as time goes on. I have learned that although it is natural to feel defeated at times or get caught up in someone or some event in our lives, if we dwell in this place for too long, we may let something amazing walk right on by.

Life has a funny way of working itself out and it is way too short to hold on to the people who do not value you or cling to the mistakes of the past. This life is about moving forward, not backward. Sometimes what we want and what we need are completely opposed to one another and that is just all there is to it. How do we know the difference? That is a tough question to answer, but I'll give it a shot based on my own experiences.

First of all, you should never have to beg for love and/or attention from someone who truly cares for you, because to those who truly care it is something you will never have to question. Words are merely words and leave the lips of the deceitful just the same as they do from those with good intentions. The difference is that those with good intentions validate those words with actions. We all make mistakes and behave in ways we are not proud of, so I am not saying you should dismiss anyone who doesn't put you on a pedestal - that's a bit extreme!

It is okay to give someone a chance to make amends, but be careful about letting them off too easy. The word sorry is over used and over appreciated in my opinion and it is again just a word. True amends are made by going the extra mile, not just apologizing for what you did wrong. The day you embrace this knowledge you will find that you hold not only yourself, but everyone-else in your life to a higher standard.

And I assure you, when you least expect it, you will cross paths with someone you may have never seen coming, had you been too busy chasing after someone else. And the same advice is relevant with circumstances too. Just like people, opportunities will come and go in your life, you just have to try your best to ensure you are going after the right ones and not spending too much time trying to make the wrong ones into something they are not.

We are all in this together... some of us just weren't meant to walk next to one another.

A Never Ending Journey

Lost within a moment...
Broken are these thoughts.
There seems to be a stranger in my head these days.
With the striking resemblance to the girl I was long ago.
Crushing the assurance of yesterday.
Casting shadows on the truth.
It is the over thinker.

The second guesser.
The frightened.
I've battled these
demons before...
The unknowing,
The insecure.
The doubt.
I turned away once
before.
And so I shall again.
To overcome
triumphant.
Re-centered,
And self-assured.
Oh what a never ending
journey...
These challenges,
This life.

Confidence

Here I stand in the corner of my life
Yelling at the top of my lungs, but no one seems to hear me…
What if I were to scream? Would they notice me then?
Soft spoken and shy
I cower from societal normalcy
What is "normal" anyway?
I prefer to be unique
Although sometimes it can be awfully lonely
I am confident
For someday I will find my clan
And until then
I stand alone in the corners of my mind

When Will I Be Free

Tears roll down my face
As the little voice in my head begins to banter with positivity
An enemy from long ago rears its ugly head once again
When will it go away
When will I be free
Self-doubt and ridicule pick apart my self-esteem
As I struggle with self-image and expectation
A battle I keep fighting
But never seem to win
I know freedom lies in accepting
where I am
Who I am
And all I've yet to be
Yet on days like these.
I find it hard to keep the fire going
As this old familiar pain
Pours heavily on my heart
I long for the day
When I am no longer my worst
enemy

Allusive

The quiet makes me quiver
As I slowly fade to dust
No one is listening
No one is here

I am alone

Caught between a memory
And the hope for something more
Reaching out for comfort
Yet allusive in my words
If only
I possessed the courage to say
I need a friendly shoulder
Before I lose control
This world that I exist in
Is shaking at its core

And I

Just a lonely traveler
Stranded beyond the physical
And something in between

Broken language
Breeds bitter tears
As I surrender to the dark

Disappointed
Broken hearted
But wiser just the same

For I have had this feeling
Too many times before
So familiar
Like razors on my skin

And so
I disappear
Running from the prospect
Of another broken wing

Confusion

Sometimes the thing you don't want to hear is exactly the thing you need to hear in order to find clarity in an otherwise confusing situation. I think we all keep things to ourselves that we think may hurt someone else, but is that really the best course of action? I am not talking about little things like keeping the fact that your friend's new haircut is less than flattering to yourself. I am talking about the big stuff...life changing stuff.

Our time on this earth is so precious and any time spent worrying about something that could have otherwise been prevented is a waste. The truth is that honesty is what really sets you free. Seeing someone's true colors can change your opinion of them in an instant. An instant that may never have come if they had always stayed hidden. People in our lives come and go, that is just the cold hard truth about life. Not everyone is going to stay your friend and not every relationship is going to work out.

We see things the way we want to see them. We hear things the way we want to hear them. And when our expectations are less than what we hoped, we are left wondering why. We pick apart the situation and ourselves. When the truth is right there in front of us.
 It is humbling to find that you have been a pawn in someone's deceitful game of cat and mouse. However, the knowledge of this can be just what you needed to move on. Sadness and confusion becomes anger and from this comes strength. You no longer spend your time wasted on someone that doesn't deserve it. And when faced with the same situation again, the memories of the pain is what keeps you from making the same mistake.

So the next time you think you are doing someone a favor by keeping the cold hard truth to yourself, think about that.

Are you really helping them or just delaying the inevitable pain that could set them free?

Confusingly Perturbed

I find myself disturbed
Confusingly perturbed
Delinquently denied
A child left behind

My lost and found
My hopes left drown
Lost world
Lost love
My life

Ms. Misunderstood

Lonely was the language of my heart.
So please forgive me when I don't know what to say
How to act
Or how to play
With you.
I'm not used to being cared for
Understood
Or even wanted for that matter.
These feelings of affection and kindness
Frighten me
For I treasure them all too much
Craving them in the dark
Longing for them in the day.
I never thought I wanted this
But now...
I can't think of anything
I've ever wanted more
Than you.

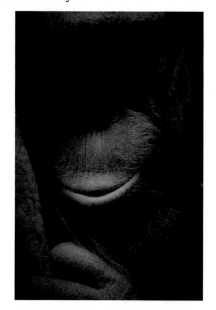

My Gypsy Man

A gypsy man once held my hand
And said he knew my future.
He moaned and hummed a gypsy hum
And tickled me with a feather.
He closed his eyes and with a sigh...
He gasped and choked and staggered,
"Your life is gone, yet you're still here! I'm puzzled as to why though?"
I laughed at him and then I smiled
"Well that explains my sleepless nights
And horrific cries for mercy."
I must have been a bad, bad girl
This life's not life, but hell you see
With hurt I burn eternally.

Denial

A few years ago, I went to see a counsellor about some deeply painful abandonment issues I was dealing with and he told me that we should treat the loss of a friendship or relationship as we do that of those who pass away. In many cases, as in death, we are not given the closure we so desperately crave and if we do not find a way to work through that on our own, it leaves a hole in our lives that we continually try to fill. Sometimes the closure we need is not available and therefore it is up to us to find a way to move on without it. Easier said than done of course, but such is life.

Everyone experiences loss in different ways and for me being left behind or disregarded was something I experienced at a very early age, which is perhaps why it has become my downfall. And I am not referring to the distance that can sometimes grow between two people. I have many friends that I don't talk to on a regular basis, but it doesn't mean I care for them any less or vice versa. We all get busy and caught up in life, but if one of us were to reach out, the other would always be there no matter how much time has passed. I value those people more than they will ever know. Their love is what gets me through in the darkest of hours, even if their presence is not always there.

What I am referring to are those that lack the common decency to clarify their reasoning before simply throwing away a long-time friendship. Especially, when you are not able to find a reason for them doing so. The ones you thought you meant something to. Those you talk to on a regular basis, confide in and who never gave you a reason to doubt their loyalty until one day, they just walk away with no explanation. Those are the ones that make it hard to open up again to anyone. They are the people that remind you why you have always found it so hard to trust people when they say they care.

Over and over, it seems to feel like breaking down the walls seems to only end in pain. I don't know about you, but I have a tendency to internalize the cruel actions of another as a reflection of myself or as a result of something I have done, but in almost all cases that is simply not true. Rationally, I know that, but the damage to my heart and loss of faith in humanity seemed for so long to be irreversible. It would be wonderful if everyone treated others with the amount of respect they deserve, but that is simply not how the world operates.

Perhaps the reason I could never treat those people the way they treated me is because I have been on the other end of it so many times that it has almost broke me. I could never live with myself if I knew I was responsible for inflicting that much pain on another person.

We don't know what others are experiencing at any given time and our callousness could be what sends them over the edge. And besides, is it really that hard to be kind?

I would never ask anyone to stay in my life if they did not wish to do so, but it is simply inhuman to toss someone aside like they mean nothing and with no explanation.

If you are experiencing this in your life, I urge you to review the five stages of grief, it may help you find a way to find closure in an otherwise open ended situation. Denial is most commonly listed as the first stage of grief. It is the survival mechanism.

When the focus becomes trying to get through the day despite feeling overwhelmed and in many cases numb. You don't want to believe that this person would treat you like this. You don't want to believe you were once again fooled.

It is dehumanizing and heartbreaking to think that someone you have allowed yourself to be vulnerable with has no regard for your feelings. Especially when it is so hard to open up to people in the first place. This a stage I know very well, as evident in the poetry within this chapter.

Pleasurable Discomfort

Wounded, she drove.
Into the night, she sped.
There was no looking back now.
For something had come over her just moments before.
As she turned the key, put down her phone and lit her last cigarette
The painful reality of this distance took hold.
Wiping a tear from her cheek
She tried to pretend it didn't matter.
She didn't care.
It didn't hurt.
But it did.
And it scared her.
She was here again
In this space
Of pleasurable discomfort.
One that time has proven,
Only leads to damage.
And the disappointment,
Of yet another failure.
To be brave, would be her triumph.
But she fears, the risk too great.
For her heart,
Has no more room for stitches.
And her mind no place for doubt.
For once…
She thought,
It would be nice to be the prize,
Instead of the one fighting for it.
And so...
Wounded, she drove.
Into the night, she sped.
Trying to pretend it didn't matter.
She didn't care.
It didn't hurt.
But it does.

I pretend

I miss you
Even though I shouldn't
I love you
And I fear I always will
I am broken
Although I may seem strong

Each day I struggle
Each day I pretend
I don't miss you
I don't love you

And everything's okay

Moonlight Dreams

Blue is the haze that sets upon this night
Alone with my thoughts far within the deepness of the dark
What was once a place I held secret
Hidden behind stonewalls and barbed
wire
Is now the heart of the wounded
Tattered, torn and bruised
Mend it will
But for now
Under the glow of the moon
All I wish to do
Is fade into the dream of a better
tomorrow
One without disappointment
Miscommunication
And unspoken words
A shred of hope buried under the ruble of
a broken heart
Just enough to sooth
In the lonely midnight hour
A moonlight dream
Of what could have been
And the denial
That it will ever be

Disappointment

I think one of the most difficult parts of growing up is finding the strength to pull the skeletons from your closet. It would seem so much easier to hide them away forever and leave the past in the past, but in everything we have done that we are not proud of, there is a little piece of ourselves hidden among the ashes. I hear a lot of people say they are broken and there is great beauty in that. But, what if we don't have to be broken? What if there was a way to put ourselves back together?

When I first started writing my memoir, I remember it being very painful at times. Revisiting memories that I had selectively forgotten in order to save my own sanity. As soon as I opened the door to my childhood, they all came rushing back and the wall of security I had built began tumbling down around me. It was from within one of the lowest moments of my life that I found my greatest strength. One by one, I confronted the residual emotional patterns that I had built up during those years. The feelings of disappointment, neglect, abandonment, and loss. The root of my constant need for approval and co-dependency. My fear of love or the loss there of. Piece by piece, I began putting myself back together. Until I came to a place of great appreciation for all that I had experienced. I was a new person the day I finished the first chapter and even more so as I wrote the final page.

The moment my mother left me, something in me changed. Something it took years of reflection to understand. I spent a great deal of my life beyond that point feeling as though I always had to prove something to someone. In the earlier years it was proving to everyone else that I was not my mother. Showing them that I could conquer anything and everything she couldn't.

Needless to say, it led me down a road where I did a lot of things I am not necessarily proud of. Things...the majority of the people in my life have no idea I did and for that matter would have a hard time believing I ever could do. Up until now, I was not ready to share these things with anyone, let alone the whole world. But you know what?

The person I am today is not just the result of all of the good things I have done. It is also and maybe more so, everything I have done that I am not proud of, those little pieces of myself hidden among the ashes.

I am living proof that in this life, we are not bound by the mistakes of our past or the circumstances placed on us by others.

And therefore, if telling my story is an inspiration to even just one, it's worth it.

Growing Apart

It has been said
Actions speak louder than words
Their mounting disrespect
And overwhelming disappointment
In a person I thought I knew
As neglect builds
A wedge begins to grow
What was once the strongest of
bonds
Has begun to fall away
There is no mutual benefit
In a friendship of convenience
When one truly cares
The time is made
And so it would seem
Our time together is coming to an end
For I am not one to tolerate
This constant disregard
I am worth much more than this
I hope someday you can find a way to understand
I am not weary and I am not weak
I am simply out of place
Just a shadow on the wall of someone else's life
It's time that I move forward
It's time to let me go

Broken Memories of a Delicate Feeling

If you'd asked me why I bother, I'd tell you honestly I don't know.
It should be common knowledge by now that I am not meant to lead a normal life.
Nor am I meant to love or be loved in the usual way.
I am a prisoner to my own mind these days.
A fault that is purely my own.
For I thought perhaps something had changed.
For a moment it felt like maybe there was more to this life than just being strange.

But...thinking like that will only leave you weary
And I am already exhausted by the hope for something more.
Insulted by my own foolish blunder.
Angry at myself for acting against my better judgement.
Allowing myself to be vulnerable.

After all, I should know better than that.

Enough

The glitter has all faded,
The will to fight has fled.
Laying in the darkness,
Wishing for the end.
Tired of pretending,
He didn't break her heart.
His disregard,
So painful,
Only one choice remains,
To give up the fight.
Exhausted by these memories,
Swimming in her head.
Broken promises,
And the hope that someday,
She would be enough.
If not to him, to someone.
It's just a flicker now...
That light dangling at the end
of the tunnel.
For it once held the prospect of
something better,
A reason to keep on fighting.
But now...
Now it is simply a reminder,
Of oh so many failed attempts.
To matter, just a little...
To be loved.

My Mistake

I awoke today at 4 AM
Cringing at the prospect of another day
I am exhausted I thought
Lost
Wandering through the darkness of my mind
Sleep was my only peace
From this cloak of sanity
I must abide
For I am cracked you see
Jagged
These edges on my heart, embellished with scars
From lovers of the past
Those who taught me
Just how worthless
One can make you feel
Thank you for reminding me that I mean nothing
For a moment, I actually thought you cared

My mistake

Not Today

I had the chance to see you today
But I knew I couldn't take it
Couldn't fake it
Not today

Wasted

Whipped by selfless wonder
And torn in two by hate
Used by endless kindness
A lifeless little waste

Sleep

I used to think there were never enough hours in the day,
But these days it seems there are too many.
Morning comes like clockwork,
Forcing me to face the pain I hold within.
It used to be easy, hiding behind this facade,
But these days, I struggle.
Begging for nightfall before the sun has fully risen in the sky,
Craving the peace that only sleep can bring.
The nights are becoming shorter now,
With the swallow of every pill.
An act of self-preservation.

For I fear if sleep does not come soon,
Courage may be lost and all hope abandoned in facing another day.

Ambitions of Despair

Soon this will be over
This now...
Soon to be a moment in the past.
Those hurtful words that cut so deep
Their painful moisture dripping down my cheeks
The Darkness.
So little light...
In times like these.
Serious thoughts weigh heavy on my mind
As thick black hate courses through my veins
Slowly the anger subsides
And I am left here
Feeling weak
In this overwhelming defeat
In times like these.
Searching for strength in solitude
For soon it will all be over
This now...
Soon to be a moment of the past
This present...A fading memory

No Tomorrow

One day there will be no chance to make amends,
Hold the ones you love,
Or remind them that you care.
One day the shoulder they needed,
May be the one thing you wish you had not withheld.
It could have made the difference,
Given them a reason to stay,
But you'll never know.
Because for them,
There is no tomorrow.

I stumbled upon this in my travels last year in Tennessee and it brought tears to my eyes....so beautiful.
And if you will notice on the plaque to the right the date of dedication is listed as September 16th. Which just so happens to be, my birthday.
In that moment, I felt as though I was being hugged by the heavens.

Confident Reality

I reside here in confidence
Strength and resilience my security
A peaceful place to rest my bones
No longer questioning myself
Void of all impatience
For that which has yet to be
Content with being me
And thankful
Oh so thankful
For the life I'm meant to lead

Winds of Change

Sheltered in the warmth of this new reality
A place of freedom and gratitude
I am changed
For I have freed myself of expectation
And opened my heart and mind to all that has yet to come
I have no fear
I hold no regrets
Held beneath this bright blue sky
I welcome the gifting winds of change
Cleansing thoughts of uncertainty
As they bring to me all that I have yet to know
The comfort of sun upon my face
Tickling my skin with its warm embrace
Reminding me of the power held within the unknown
Oh how I welcome these winds of change

Thoughts on the Bus

This world
Her undeniable beauty
Her soot, her grime
Her perpetual strength
So easily overlooked

Embrace this

As only you know how
Then you and only you
Shall be the wiser

Anger

I believe anger is a self-explanatory and extremely necessary emotion in healing. It is okay to feel angry with the person that hurt you, disregarded you or made you feel as though you were meaningless in some way. We must embrace this stage wholeheartedly if we are to move forward. After all, it is impossible to forgive someone when you still have anger in your heart. And forgiveness (even if they are not deserving of it) is the end goal. Not for them, but in order for you to move on.

There was a time in my life when I was afraid to stand up for myself or even speak my mind for that matter. Looking back, I allowed myself to feel such misery. All because I was worried about losing someone I wasn't even destined to be with. All those people I compromised myself for and even the one that I didn't, left me behind anyway. The knowledge that I would always be around made it easy for them to brush me aside until they needed something from me once again.

After my last broken heart, something snapped inside me. I realized that all the pain I was feeling, I brought on myself by once again being too available to someone who merely needed me for the moment. Now that the moment had passed him, he no longer needed my comfort and he never give me a second thought or any thought for that matter.

I realized, I was broken inside, but he wasn't. I loved him so much that I never stopped to ask myself if he ever really felt the same about me. If only I would have realized sooner that I was merely a comfort to a friend and nothing more, then maybe I could have avoided all those sleepless nights. It was in this moment of revelation when everything changed. I was tired of sitting on a shelf waiting to be needed and I decided I was not going to do it anymore. Instead, I would give putting myself first a try for once and move on with my life.

Collateral Damage

Callus was the heart of the man she tried to love.
Careless, the mind of a friend she tried to understand.
Broken was her spirit, the day he slipped away.
Not for the pain of losing love, but rather the reality that it was never really there.
Those neat little words, dripping ever so delicately from his tongue.
As the desire for truth overshadowed its nonexistence.
Their many moments together, when the world would seem to fade away.
Are now just memories she longs to forget.
The connection between them that she once felt was unmistakable,
She suddenly realized was all in her head.
Perhaps foolishly, she thought their history meant something,
That she meant something, to him.
But now that time has passed and reflection taken hold,
All hope for him has faded into dust.
Those arms that once held comfort,
Hold nothing more than disappointment now.

And the piercing reminder, that he never really cared.
Not really, not for her. It is all much clearer now.
She was merely a convenient relief for him, after a time of heartbreak and loss.
A familiar pleasure to pass the time.

Nothing more, than collateral damage, in his search for something better.

The Man behind the Mask

Of all the monsters I've encountered
I never thought it would be you.
To take me so high into the sky,
Just to let go when I needed you the most.
To your kindness I was a fool,
For I never imagined,
I was not safe with you.
I thought I knew the man behind the mask,
The beautiful stranger underneath.
But now I see,
You meant the world to me,
And I,
I meant nothing to you.

I Will Not Be Broken

Anger courses through my veins
As disappointment drips slowly
down my face
The sadness is maddening
For I refuse to be broken
Not again, not this time.
I own this misconception
For it is mine alone
Acting against my better judgement
A familiar mistake
That always seems to leave me
bruised.
I had hoped that this was different
That maybe, just once...
There was more to this life
Than simply existing
Alone.
Perhaps it is valuable
This realization that nothing lasts
forever
Life's piercing reminder to appreciate those moments of pure vulnerability
For they are few and far between.
And growing less likely with every passing day.
Opening up, giving my all
Is not something I do easily
Nor an act I reserve for the common.
But even the exceptional
Have their doubts
Or so it would seem.
My defenses are rising
The walls rebuilding
In one last attempt to step away before it's too late.
For I refuse to be broken
Not again, not this time.

Fighting the Darkness

It's cold here
Deep within the pit of my despair
It's lonely here
Backed within the corner of my rage
I can feel it more strongly now
So much stronger than before
The resentment
The disappointment
The darkness
This shattered reality
I am forced to bare

An overwhelming sorrow for all that is
lacking
Followed by the overwhelming shame for
feeling ungrateful for all that I have
It is in times such as these
As I lay here alone with my thoughts
That I find myself consumed with longing
Longing for all that I have lost and all that
never was
I begin to wonder
I think about lost love and why it never
seems to work
Even when it feels so right
It ends up being so wrong
And I worry
Will I ever find truth?
Will anyone ever mean what they say?
Will anything ever be real?

My heart beats heavily within my chest
Weighing me down with every breath
Tears journey down my cheeks
Shedding painful memories of the past
In this moment
I am weak
In this moment
I am human
And in this moment, that's okay

Silly Little Optimist

You silly little optimistic girl. Did you really think it would be different?
No one will ever love you.
Not with their whole heart at least.

Perhaps the mystery in your eyes will lead them to ponder...
To wonder...
What it would be like...
To love you.
But as with everything, that will surely fade.
You were not meant to be loved my dear.
There is no peace for you here.
No happiness.
No joy.
Loneliness; the only thing that's real.
So walk or better yet, run
Far away from it all.
Go dark
Go distant
They won't notice
Here today, gone tomorrow
You never meant a thing to them.

What's Your Story?

Faintly in the distance, I can see a glimmer of hope.
A glimmer of love and security in this crazy world.
Crowded by doubt and needful resolution, it struggles to come to surface.
Brighter days lie ahead, but we must have faith in their existence.
Through dark clouds and sorrow, comes wisdom and strength.
Strength to keep on fighting and wisdom to learn from our pain.
In life we lead a story.
Whether it be a tragedy, a drama or a comedy is only for us to decide.

Depression

Looking back on my life the years that formed me seem to be, in most instances, a blur. Their significance blind to the hopeless soul I was back then. They were of the most influential moments of my life and yet they are the farthest from the reality in which I currently exist. Perhaps it is the loneliness I once found an uncomfortable comfort in that disallows the appreciation of a time in its absence. And so, it is the loneliness to which I cling. After all, for the majority of my life it was the only real constant I had ever known.

I have always considered myself to be broken and more importantly, that being broken was far from beautiful. I have come to learn, I was extraordinarily wrong. The most beautiful people in this world are the broken, the wounded and the left behind. For so long, we just simply never had a voice. A sounding board on which to express that which is not modern opinion and/or comprehension.

We are all beautiful. Every scar is something we've overcome, a wound healed and perhaps a lesson learned. They should not be judged harshly, but rather celebrated as a triumph of strength and accomplishment. You've faced something, regardless of its intensity and you have overcame.

I am not of the masses, the typical or the usual. I do not fit within the confines of the realities of most. And so, for so long…I did not feel as though I would survive. I have spent my days living on the outskirts, never getting too close or letting anyone far enough in to see the damage I try so hard to hide.

And thus, I've struggled in this world to be anything but unusual. Fitting in was survival. Being part of the pack was what I thought would give my life meaning. A purpose in a world that seemed strange and overwhelming. And when I didn't fit in as a normal would, I found myself once again in a depressing spiral of discontent. Over and over again, I found myself in the same downward spiral until it eventually became a comfort. I was so used to being in pain that the torment became my preservation. And thus each day became harder than the next.

Now, some would simply shrug this off as life. After all, we all have ups and downs, perhaps those who experience the feelings I described above are of the hyperbolic, melodramatic breed. And I'll give you that there is always going to be a certain amount of crazy we just can't account for. But what if in some cases it's more than that?

How many of you know someone who suffers from depression? I mean really think about it. There are those that have life experiences that cause a low and an understandable spout of immense sadness, which is life.

But I would bet that almost every person reading this knows at least one person, for whom it goes beyond that. It is not something that is talked about enough. It is one of those subjects that can sometimes get dismissed as if it is a cop out for the weak. But it's not. It's real. And it's about time we remove the veil of shame attached to it and understand it for what it truly is.

Those who, for lack of a better word, suffer from this said affliction are not at all weak. Quite the opposite actually. They are the warriors. They are the ones who wake each day with a mountain on their chest. Their heart as heavy as their mind, but still they find a way to rise. They push forward through the normal life struggles with an ocean of sadness on their back as if it is usual practice. It's different for everyone, but that is the best generalization I can muster.

Personally, my best explanation is that each day for me feels like a prison. I wake each morning, battling myself, pushing against a current of self-doubt and hesitancy as I rise to face the day. 'I am not alone' I tell myself and all be it true, I still have to force myself to believe it. Every morning, of every day, I have to fight, with the one person I should trust the most, myself. Every affirmation of love brings a feeling of irrational inadequacy rooted in a childhood of indifference that I just can't seem to escape.

It is in moments like these, those wee hours of the night, that it almost seems easier. Maybe it is because much of the world is asleep. Less of those to judge. Those who may never understand, just how vacant one can feel when faced with their own reflection.

I see so much of her in me, yet I'm not really sure I even know who that is. And therefore, sometimes, really most of the time, I'm still struggling to find myself amongst what seems like a lifetime of never knowing what was real. I don't know if I'll ever figure it out. You know, genuinely find the solution to healing the misery of the past, but what I do know is…I'm not alone. And neither are you.

To Be Unbroken

I wonder sometimes…
What it would be like
To wake each day,
Without the darkness
Casting shadows on the light.
To feel safe,
For more than just a moment.
To be unbroken,
And not just for pretend.
That's the thing about depression...
Even on the brightest of days,
There will always be a cloud... a storm,
Hovering above.
Waiting at the ready to unleash its wrath.
And each day,
We fight.
We overcome.
In the hopes that someday,
We will find our place in the sun.

Somewhat Wicked Life

These days,
I find great comfort in being alone.
In a world filled with monsters,
It all seems such a pointless charade.
One I no longer desire to fight.
Not for anyone,
Not anymore.
I've no need for the notion,
That I'd ever be chosen.
For it will only end in pain.
And so, I find myself treasuring the dark,
This solitude, my security,
In this somewhat wicked story of my life.

Photo courtesy of Krista Boettcher

Happy Birthday

Today is a day much like any other
To everyone else that is.
For me today has much potential for *JOY*
But I must first navigate through the emotional baggage attached to its
creation.
I awake feeling saddened, disappointed and as I always do on this
day...missing something.
A love that will never come, a mother who left me behind and the
unworthiness I feel inside.

And so I spiral
Just for a moment
Holding the hand of *Reznor*
As I recall all that could have been
And something I will never have.
Feeling quite the wretched

Hurt

But I do not want this.
And so once I hit the bottom,
I will slowly wash it all away.

Obviously this poem was inspired by Nine Inch Nails, as was the next. I've never met
Trent Reznor, but the influence of his music has had a great impact on my life.

It is amazing how the darkness of a stranger can sometimes save you.

As I Journey Further Down the Spiral

Tip toe, tip toe, closer to the edge.
Slowly I tumble...
Down into the darkness.
Lonely are these heart strings,
That once held hope for love.
Broken are these memories,
Of old forgotten friends.
Left behind, moving on,
Never looking back.
Destined for solitude.
Unloved, unwanted and alone.

Just Sometimes

A part of me wishes I wasn't here
On this earth
Surrounded by all these humans
Misunderstood
This tragic little mess of me

A part of me wants to run away
To leave this world
Not to face another day
I am exhausted
Tired of wearing this mask
Hiding the broken pieces of my soul
Pretending that I am not falling apart
Assuring everyone else that everything is
okay
When sometimes...
It's not okay
I'm not okay
There are moments
When all I feel is hollow

Empty inside
Destroyed...Damaged
And dismembered
There are times
When all I want is to be held
To be told that I matter
Assured that I am worthy
Even if it's just for a moment
I want to feel as though
I won't always have to walk alone
But that would mean removing this
disguise
Revealing to the world
That I am among the strange
That I don't belong here
And so...
Once again
I muster up the energy to continue this masquerade
Holding it together
When all I want to do is fall apart

The Illusion of Happiness

Behind those bright green eyes
Lies darkness
Hidden behind a cheerful grin
The illusion of, a hopeful mind
The reality is, there's nothing left
No fight
No Strength
Only pain
Wrapped around a hollow shell
Of the person she used to be

Hollow

There once was a girl who took on the world.
Her heart was full, her future bright.
Oh how I miss her,
And that glimmer in her eyes.
Ripped in two by more than a few.
Until all that remained was a mile wide ditch in her chest.
She is just a hollow shell now.
Unable to love, unable to care.
Numb to this existence.
Maybe the rest of life will be less painful,
Now that she has nothing more to give, nothing more to take.
Useless to those that wish to prey on the optimistic and the bold.
For he was the one to throw the last stone.
The one that shattered the only remaining piece of her heart.

Bruised

If you knew the pain I was feeling, would it matter
If you knew that love was fading, would you pick up the phone
I trusted you and those words that slipped off your tongue
And you...you tossed me aside

It could have been different, you and I
But you...you wouldn't even try
It could have been easy, amazing, even forever
But I guess we'll never know
For I love myself much more than you
And I refuse to live in a constant state of disappointment
I am worthy of more, much more than this
Maybe you were right
Maybe I do deserve better
I cannot change the way I feel
For I fear that I will always love you
Yet in this moment, I know

The only path is
moving forward
Beyond this
Beyond you
And some day, I
hope
I can look at you
without this pain
in the pit of my
stomach
Absent of desire
And free
Free from your
love and the
memories of you

Inside Myself

It's cold here, alone with my thoughts.
Drowning in doubt, from my mind's fearful inquest.
Lonesome and drifting, as happiness fades to anguish.
I remember this feeling...
This longing, this worry
This terror that it will all go away.
I am trying to be brave, courageous
In the face of this affection.
I can feel myself shutting down, pulling back.
An all too familiar defense.
In the prevention of yet another broken heart.
The scars of the past have only just healed
Still dripping with the blood of love lost.
The pain is gone, but the memory of it remains.
And the knowledge that what I am facing, is so much greater than any
devotion of the past.
Surely the loss of which could be something from which I may never recover.
For it is something, I have never wanted more.
Rugged, raw and pure.
To be seen for all that I am and admired still.

Melancholy Snowfall

I am somber today,
Grimly wistful towards the path that lies ahead.

As the melancholy snow dances on my lips,
I am gently reminded of what no longer exists.

For it is spring now and winter shall soon be behind us.

Mournful for the sun, I find strength to shake the chill.

Emerging from the darkness, reaching eagerly towards the light.

It is only a faint glimmer, flickering with uncertainty in the distance.

I extend my hand, hoping to embrace the warmth of its presence.

Only to be drenched in regret.

Sopping and soaked, I weep.

It's moments like these that can break a person.

It's moments like these that show you what you are made of.

In a place that once felt like the end, I have found a new beginning.

Reflection

You know that feeling you get when you want something so bad you are crawling out of your skin? And the longer it takes to get it the more you seem to want it. I would like to throw out there that maybe what you want is not necessarily what you need and the reason you are not getting it is because something bigger than ourselves is intervening. I have found that when things don't turn out the way I would like them to, instead of getting frustrated, it is better to appreciate the disappointments as a way of expanding our consciousness. And the contrast of it, essential to our own personal growth.

My suggestion would be to allow ourselves to listen to those inner callings. Pay attention to the pull that we feel from some invisible intelligence, burning desire, or inner light that is constantly speaking to us. Sadly, in many cases we may chose to ignore it and find out later that we should have gone with our gut, am I right? Perhaps when you decide to start listening, your entire life can change. One with new roads that lead to new experiences and opportunities. Ones that you may have never known before.

Deep down, I think many of us feel as though we have a greater purpose, but for one reason or another we keep ourselves from finding out what that is. We tell ourselves that we are satisfied with our current condition out of fear of failure if we try to pursue another course of action. One that perhaps may mean more to us than any other we have ever encountered. This fear should be our worst enemy, not the puppet master manning our strings.

So, I challenge you to listen to that inner voice, whether it be to take a different route home, shop at a different store or simply wear something different than you had originally planned for the day. And then pay very close attention to the moments that manifest (however small they may be) as a result of doing just that. I have come to learn that if you allow your life to unfold naturally, you will naturally find your purpose and your peace. There is a time for everything, not just the positive but the opposite negative aspects as well.

I am not trying to tell you that every day is going to come up roses. There is a time for struggle, a time for pain, depression and so on, but in those moments, if you can remember that there will also be a time for joy, fulfillment and rejoice, you may be better able to grow as a person. And as you do, you get to a new place in your life where you begin to understand that it is all about balance. When you step back and keep yourself from telling others how they should live and what they should do, you begin to accept them for who and where they are. It is not your duty to control the lives of others and it puts so much unnecessary pressure on your life when you try to do so. It is one thing to care about someone and feel that you have their best interests at heart, but it is important to remember that you are viewing their situation through your own looking glass. What is best for you is not always best for them. Perhaps they need to take a wrong turn in order to learn a very valuable lesson that will serve them greatly in the future. Their life is not yours to lead, to judge or to fix. Just love them and allow their life and your own to unfold naturally.

Like many, I used to place blame on others for the way my life was. It was not until I took responsibility for my current condition that I was able to truly make a change. The point I want to drill home is that from my experience, I have found that we have the power within us to seize the opportunity in any given moment and make a change. Whatever it is that is creating stress in our lives is in itself a chance to learn, a chance to grow and a chance to change our circumstance. How you feel is a choice. You can choose to be angry or you can chose to be fulfilled and the choice you make will set the pace for all that comes next.

It is my greatest desire for you to find joy among this vast environment of negativity that can sometimes feel inescapable.

And that at the end of your days you will hold no regrets, but instead hold an enormous amount of gratitude for the life you have led.

Courageously Broken

And suddenly, it was all clear.
This is dangerous...forbidden
Outside the constructs of this world.
United, we are invincible.
Routine is the comfortable...the ordinary.
But we...we shake it up.

With fiercely ignited passion,
The kind...that just could save a
life.
The only way to truly conquer the
demon inside.

And for that, this universal force
works diligently to keep us apart.
For we hold the potential for
destruction.

Together we are reckless,
The unstoppable change feared by
the normal.

Un-empathetically driven.
Those with true purpose.

Humanity's only hope for vindication.

We are...
The courageously broken

Have You Ever?

Have you ever wished you were able to go back to a time in the past, not to change it, but simply to experience it again with all of the knowledge you now hold.
Moments you've forgotten and synchronicity you never understood.
One long winding road to the place you are now.
The person you have become.
Those twisted roots of history woven together to create your current reality.
How does it feel to know you chose this?
Every decision you have ever made has led to that which you are experiencing now.
Do you have any regrets...things you never said...and those you will never be able to say?
Has it taught you anything?
Perhaps...
That time is fleeting.
And no one knows what tomorrow will bring...

Fleeting

One by one these days go by
Drawing us further and further
From the fire.
What was once so shiny and new
Is beginning to lose its luster.
Something so easy
Turned struggle
By the mere mention of desire.

For happiness
Must be for the delusional
And love is surely a scam.
Excuses for the weak
The frightened
And some day

The justification
For the lonely

Home

Let it open, let it be,
Release this.
A dead horse driven chariot,
This stage coach, life calls fate.
Optimistic chances for pessimistic minds.
Now chanting:
Believe this, release this, proceed this.

Journey home.

Where Did You Go?

Close your eyes now
Just for a moment
Breathe in
Breathe out
Now open
Where did you go?
Who, what, when...just crossed your mind?
Was it something you've always wanted, something you could never live
without, or perhaps...something you almost had?
Someone you care for, someone you long for, someone you miss?
Was it a time in the past, the present, the future?
In that split moment of being
Where did your mind go?
More importantly
Did you want it to come back?

Too Short

I say to you now that life is too short
Too short for your grumbling and mumbling
Complaining and ungratefulness
There is a great big world out there
Beyond your whirlwind of negative thinking and greed
It is so beautiful
If you would only open your eyes to its magnificence

Pause for a moment
Just take it all in
This wonderful life that surrounds you
It's too short
Not to appreciate
Tomorrow it could vanish
Leaving today as your last
What is the legacy
That you would leave behind

Close your eyes
Listen to the sound of
life around you
Feel the breeze as it
blows across your
skin
Breathing in energy
and appreciation
Exhaling negativity
and letting go of all
that does not serve
you

Open your eyes
Now embrace this day as if it were your last.

Mindful Surrender

Bitter sweet deception consumes my mind.
As the fruit of hope dances on my tongue.
I've been here before.
Standing on the edge of this emotion.
Arms spread wide, eyes sealed tight,
And I tumbled.
Collapsing into an abyss of unrequited desire.
Left alone in the darkness.
Cold and defeated.
Reminded that perhaps, I was never meant to be loved.
And so, as the prospect of something magical returns, I hold myself away.
Trapped somewhere between love and fear.
It is a warm place, where the shadows keep my cravings for him at bay.
As the scars on my heart advise me to stay.
And stay I shall.
Locked inside the prison of my
own mind.
Conveniently disregarded.
Waiting...for someone
To fight for love.
Someone, for once
To fight...for me.

Dreamers Prayer

As I lay myself to sleep
The silence of the dark wraps tightly around my skin
Alone in my bed
Swimming in my own imagination
A fairytale of memories
Written with the deepest of regret
All feels lost, but perhaps it is not
For all that could have been and all that has yet to come
Can always be
If I only close my eyes

Inspiration

Inspiration can come from a variety of places and it is different for everyone. For me, quite obviously, I am inspired by the darkness. It is what has fueled my writing and my art for as far back as I can remember and it has allowed me to create something beautiful from tragedy and despair. I think there is this tendency to look at the mistakes and failures in our lives as purely negative things, but in understanding balance, we embrace the understanding that with negative comes positive.

When I look back on the lowest times in my life, no matter how hard it got, it was always temporary. As is everything. And when it was over, I was a better person because of it. Mistakes educate and failures are just a learning gap. One simply must learn how to bridge that gap, but how?

The first step may perhaps be as simple as believing in yourself enough to strive for personal growth. Only then will you be able to internalize your true potential. Don't let the world tell you who you are or define your purpose in this life. Know yourself, support yourself, and trust yourself. It is not a sin to be confident and it is okay to feel disappointed or discouraged at times. After all, we are only human and to be human is to encompass all the emotions inflicted on us by our surroundings.

You must also learn to free yourself from inadequacy and revel in the power you have within yourself. Although you may be flawed (we all are), you are amazing, you are beautiful and you are powerful! Even if you don't know it yet.

She Runs

Born Restless
She runs
Plotting and scheming
She runs
Unable to settle
Unable to change
She will always be
My mother, the runaway

Different Breed

My whole life I have considered myself a
different breed
A different breed of human
A different breed of women
A different breed of everything all together
I stand alone because I can
I stand alone because it's safe
I stand alone
At war with the loneliness

I love with all my heart
I feel with all my being
I am who I am
A different breed

Photo courtesy of Michael Miller

Broken Shade of Blue

Once there was a boy who promised me the world.
And for a time, I thought those big brown eyes possessed the power to light
up my soul.
But I was wrong.
He left me in the shadows, never looking back,
And for a moment, I was torn.
Barely stitched and slightly bruised, I moved forward.
Until I found myself tangled up with another.
A man with eyes the broken shade of blue.
And for a time, I could feel his affection,
Growing like a sickness under my skin.
My connection to him, like none I'd ever known.
And perhaps why, losing him was such a heavy blow.
To my ego...
His absence grew longer as the days grew cold.
Until being disregarded became normal.
And all expectations began to fade.
Just like the one before, reality had now overruled my emotions
I no longer craved his validation.
For I have been given the gift of knowledge,
That those with the best intentions are not always what they seem.
In the end, it is me that is still moving forward,
Me, whose moving on.
I am now the one, leaving something behind.

All Things Considered

All things considered, I'm doing quite well
For I am no stranger to heartbreak
Disappointment
Or failure.
When you have been let down by so many
So many times
You become quite the expert at moving forward
Drudging through the mud and the muck of empty promises
And the realization that you have once again been played the fool.

For in the end, if your actions were rooted in love
There is no reason to feel ashamed.
You simply took a chance
A chance that anyone would have taken.
The prospect of something so frighteningly real it takes your breath away.
And when you find you were wrong
It is so unbelievably painful
That for a moment it may seem like you will never rise again.
But you will.
And some day you will look back on this moment and be thankful
For the scars on your hearts
They may just be the reminder we need
To keep us from making the same mistakes

In the end there is only
you
So dust yourself off

Learn from the past
And create one hell of a
future!

Knowledge of Spirit

Throughout our lives we are faced with many challenges.
And through these experiences, we are sometimes forced to make some very difficult decisions.
Those choices, right or wrong, are all part of the journey in discovering our true selves.
The person within, who has been waiting for their moment to emerge from the shadows.

Those times when we were lost and lonely, they were there.
Waiting for our awakening.

Through emotion, they try to bridge the divide in our minds.
Only to remain a stranger within.

But one day, when we no longer find ourselves fighting against them and instead begin allowing inspired action...

Together, we become conscious.

Time that was once wasted on false hopes and disillusioned ideals is now filled with inspiration and creativity.

Be a Fool

Walk a little faster
Scream a little louder
Don't be afraid to be a fool
Fools are much wiser and braver than most
Why? Because they dare to try

They have the courage to be "weird"
To stand out in the crowd
To share their inner goof with the world
around them
Fearless

Tenacious

But above all...

True

Photos courtesy of Krista Boettcher
&
Steve Anderson

Simply Complicated

Simplicity lacks what complication fulfills
Appreciation and growth
To suffer is to give thanks
One who suffers is rarely disappointed
I am not sorry for my misfortunes
I am thankful
I give credit to my most difficult trials for making me the person I am today

I would never change my past
For it has ensured my ability to live my future

Better Days

Emptiness unravels pain
Once hidden…By better days.
A time that now lay distant.
And I,

This hollow cage of life
Consumed by nothingness.
Left here by a romance overwhelmed with insanity.
I've stated my case
And planned my escape
A journey into loneliness
With simple courage as my guide.
On a path …To better days!

Days like These

On days like these
I wish you were here
Nothing specific needed
I just wish you were here

Your presence alone makes me smile
Your contagious laugh
Your free spirit
And your love
So much love
Not many have a bond like ours
You are my truest of friends

M'Lady by all accounts
I am missing you today
Missing you so much
And thanking the creative
That you are in my life
Although we are apart
Your presence is always in my
heart

Enchanted Mirror

This life
A gift

Filled with unimaginable possibilities
And endless wonder

Gratitude
The path to freedom

A simple act of appreciation
Leads to fulfillment

Reserved

Deep in my heart
There will always be a special place for you
More than you know
More than you'll ever understand
I will love you
Till the end of my days
For as long as I walk this earth
You will always be the one who…
Showed me how to love again
And for that,
I am eternally grateful

Willow Why Do You Weep?

Sweet willow
Why do you weep?
You're standing so proud
Branches steady, leaves gleaming
I thank you for your shade
Be strong little willow
There's no need to cry
I shall visit soon
But for now it's goodbye

A Different Kind of Life

I hold no grudges
Nor dwell on the past
I burn no bridges
Or plot my revenge
There is no room for hate in my heart
Or regrets...in my life
For I have learned
The meaning of the struggle
The importance of the pain
And for all of this I am thankful
Grateful
For this resulting strength
And a different kind of life

The Taste of Being Human

Dripping lips of poison tattoo my skin, as they graze along the caverns of an old and weary heart.
Its walls encrusted with the agony of darkness, misery and despair.
Built from the bricks of tragedy, sealed with scars and pounded together by the bruises of the past.
Crumbling ever slightly, as anticipation...and...its warming sensation begin to make me quiver.
Oh how I love the shiver, the shudder, this glimmer...of hope.
A momentary lapse of apprehension that will surely desecrate me further, but I hold no regrets.
I have no desire for the antivenom.
For I wish to revel in the agony of this destruction.
To suffocate beneath the feelings of pleasure, surrender to those hands delicately tracing my skin.
The precious rarity of the undeniable chemistry between us awakens me.
In this fleeting bitter sweet rendezvous I no longer feel numb, no longer lay stagnant; no longer walk alone.
And for that, I shall sacrifice the light for even just a taste of being human.

Playing With Knives

It tickles and prickles.
Gliding slowly along my skin.
The crispness of the blade piercing my flesh.
The need is growing stronger,
The yearning taking hold.
I desire to be damaged,
Fearing only he may know the way...
I like it.
How I long to be driven mad with passion,
To be taken. Without warning.
Smothered and subdued,
By the one who once held my heart.
His fetish my reflection,
Shared darkness our bond.
For wicked is his poison,
That dances on my lips.
Drizzled bits of ecstasy,
Dripping ever so delicately over my tongue.
How I wish to find him hiding,
Somewhere away in the dark.
Ready and willing,
To give up the fight.
To prove me wrong, but he won't.
To show up unannounced, disturb my foundation, unsettle my core.
But he won't.
And that's okay.
I hold no hope for romance,
After all, I'm not a child.
For the eyes of a man can be telling,
And the words of a man deceiving.
To him, I am no more than familiar.
A comfort.
A friend.
A willing party,
Away from the war.
Another broken soul,
With whom to shed the mask.
And besides,
I've never found a lover,
Man enough, to tame this wild.

Dark Heaven

Bound and raw I wait,

In exquisite anticipation...

Of your torture.

Lost in the darkness,

I quiver.

As the vastness of my skin,

Craves...

Your damage.

Destiny

The pages of my life seem to turn faster these days.
Each word spilling off my tongue in sweet anticipation of the next.
There is a flow to my story that was ever so absent before
Strength resides in patience, where fear was once so prevalent
Fate is now my beacon; a light to guide my way...
To destiny.

Hope

As a little girl, I had grand dreams of my future. I hoped for success in life and love with the outcome of only pure happiness. I spent years trying to overcome the turmoil of my past and make it into this blissful existence I was sure to be the reward for all this stress. I had always thought if I was a good person (kind, generous and loving) that the life I dreamed of would be inevitable.

Boy was I wrong! The biggest lesson in life that I've learned is that the fairy tales of a little girl are just those... fairy tales. There is no "night and shining armor" and good does not always prevail. In fact, good usually ends up the one shafted by the strong will of evil. For someone as strong-minded as myself this was a hard reality to swallow. Finding out that I needed to comprise the dreams I've held for so many years and simply disregard the rest of them was madding!

I needed to appreciate the life I had, whether it was the one I hoped for or not! Life doesn't always turn out the way you want it to, but that doesn't mean you can't enjoy it. This isn't a childhood story or uplifting movie...it's just life and whether or not it is the one I wanted, it's the one I have. I could spend every waking moment sulking about the things I'm missing or I can focus on the blessings right in front of me and the hope for better days to come.

There can be no perfection in an imperfect world, but that's the beauty of it all. You never know what the future holds. I dreamed of being a writer since I was a child and I was told many times that it was just a pipe dream. Something only the most talented could achieve and in all likelihood that wouldn't be me, but I never gave up hope and neither should you.

About a Girl

Once upon a time there was a girl
A girl who dreamed of grandeur
A world beyond her circumstance
A place of peace and security
Absent of fear and doubt.
Filled with inspiration
Flowing with ideas
She wrote
And she wrote
Recording each delicious morsel
In anticipation for the next.
Notebook after notebook
Her emotions filled the pages

Until one day it was no longer enough
She wanted more
The urge to share her experiences with the world
And so she began a record
Hoping one day she may use these words to inspire the world
To encourage
To empower
That day has finally come.
This once young and struggling writer, as of today, is now a published
author.
Living proof, you should never give up on your dream

Life After Love

It is such a beautiful moment
When the clouds begin to clear
And the sun shines brightly down the path to
tomorrow
Just think
A week ago, you
were wallowing in
disappointment
Crippled by
another broken
heart

A pain so deep
You thought you'd never recover
But much to your surprise
You did
Your life is not over
Your ego just a little bruised
For the love for yourself is much greater now than
ever before
There is no need to feel foolish
For we all put too much faith in others sometimes
You simply loved with your soul
And that is nothing to be ashamed of
It is childish for one to play games with another's
heart
And in the end they are the fool
For the broken hearted grow stronger
While they remain the same
Alone

Pause

Poisoned by time
Or lack there of
Always running
Never resting
...Pause...
Reconnect
And breathe
Refreshing the
mind
Reopening the heart
This life can wait
For you to be ready
Smile
You are in control

Final Thoughts

To anyone feeling lost,

You are not alone. Your feelings are valid and not meant to be understood by anyone but you. Your heart will heal when it's ready and only you can decide when it is time to move on.

You are not obligated to explain yourself for needing time alone with your thoughts or for anything for that matter.

It is okay to be selfish and even a little frivolous at times.

You are not perfect, but neither is anyone else.

You are going to make mistakes. Sometimes the same ones, over and over again.

Go easy on yourself. Being alive can be challenging and unexpected. You are only doing the best you can with what you have and that is all you have within your power to do.

Don't be afraid to be vulnerable. I know you have wounds deeper than most, but you will never find a way to heal them, if you don't at least try. And most importantly, find a way to love yourself.

Even if it takes a life time. You deserve it.

_____

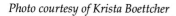

Photo courtesy of Krista Boettcher

If you or someone you know needs help finding crisis resources, please visit or call one of the services below. You don't have to do it alone.

Crisis Text Line
https://www.crisistextline.org/
Text HOME to 741741

National Suicide Prevention Lifeline:
https://suicidepreventionlifeline.org/
1-800-273-8255.

About the Author

Tiffany Rochelle, also known as Insane Roots was born in Pennsylvania in 1982, the first and only daughter of a very misguided women living under an assumed alias and a supposedly deceased father. Although her mother was her primary guardian for most of her childhood, she spent a great deal of time separated from her during her many incarcerations. After a serious car accident when Tiffany was a child where she suffered a compound leg fracture and broken collar bone, she was taken in to foster care by her godparents and her mother was arrested once again on a long list of charges.

After several years, her mother was released in to the custody of her adopted parents in Illinois and Tiffany was sent to meet her. Over the next few years, she lived here off and on between her mother's additional incarcerations, marriages and five year disappearance at the start of Tiffany's freshman year of high school. Shortly after graduating, Tiffany moved to Seattle, Washington where attended the University of Washington and obtained a B.A. in Psychology.

In 2016, she published the first in a series of memoirs recounting the many adventures of her childhood, Insane Roots: The Adventures of a Con-Artist and Her Daughter with Morgan James Publishing. And she is currently working on the second installment, Insane Roots: The Missing Pieces with an estimated release date in the fall of 2020.

Her hope is that these character pieces will offer encouragement and empowerment to those reading to embrace life's challenges as lessons in overcoming its many obstacles.
Her ability to maintain a positive outlook and find strength in an otherwise dark and chaotic upbringing, rather than let it damage her, has allowed her to become the wildly ambitious and highly motivated entrepreneur she is today.

The Poetry of Emotion

An Insane Roots Series
Tiffany Rochelle

Made in the USA
Middletown, DE
01 May 2023

29837591R00060